The History o

Shamrocks and Sagas

Emerald Origins: Unveiling Ireland's Prehistoric Foundations

In the quiet whispers of time, Ireland's prehistoric origins remain shrouded in mystery and wonder. The verdant landscapes of this island hold secrets that harken back to the dawn of human civilization. Long before the written word, Ireland's story unfolded through the imprints left in the earth, the tools crafted by early hands, and the remnants of ancient cultures that thrived upon this fertile land.

To journey into Ireland's prehistory is to step into a world that defies our modern comprehension. Archaeological evidence suggests that as far back as 10,000 BCE, Mesolithic hunter-gatherers roamed the landscape, exploiting its resources for sustenance. These early inhabitants relied on a combination of hunting, fishing, and foraging, and their life was intimately tied to the rhythms of the natural world.

As time flowed onward, the Neolithic era emerged, marking a significant shift in human history. Around 4000 BCE, Ireland's inhabitants began transitioning from a nomadic existence to settled farming communities. The cultivation of crops like barley and wheat and the domestication of animals such as cattle altered the course of society, enabling larger populations to thrive.

Monuments like Newgrange stand as testaments to the Neolithic people's ingenuity. Newgrange, a passage tomb that predates the Egyptian pyramids, showcases the remarkable architectural feats of these early communities.

Its precisely aligned passage captures the rising sun's rays during the winter solstice, revealing a deep understanding of astronomy and spirituality.

The Bronze Age, spanning from around 2500 BCE to 500 BCE, marked another epoch of transformation. Ireland's inhabitants, now equipped with advanced metallurgical techniques, forged tools, weapons, and ornamental objects from this lustrous material. Hillforts dotted the landscape, revealing the emergence of social hierarchies and fortified settlements for protection.

The Iron Age further deepened Ireland's societal complexity. Celtic tribes, known for their distinctive artistry and oral traditions, began to exert their influence on the island. The Celts introduced intricate metalwork, illuminated manuscripts, and the Gaelic language, which still resonates in modern Ireland.

The transition from prehistory to recorded history is marked by the arrival of the Romans in Britain, indirectly influencing Ireland through trade and cultural exchange. However, it wasn't until the early Christian period that written records began to chronicle the island's history. The spread of Christianity, often attributed to St. Patrick, melded ancient Celtic beliefs with the teachings of the new faith, creating a unique cultural tapestry that endures to this day.

In unveiling Ireland's prehistoric foundations, we uncover a tapestry woven with threads of innovation, adaptation, and interconnectedness with the land. The story of Ireland's early inhabitants invites us to imagine their lives, to walk in their footsteps across time's vast expanse, and to acknowledge the profound impact they had on shaping the island's destiny. The next chapters in this narrative will continue to unravel the threads that bind the ancient past to the dynamic present, revealing the layers of history that have shaped the Emerald Isle into the vibrant nation it is today.

Celtic Tapestry: Tracing the Arrival and Influence of the Celts

In the intricate mosaic of Ireland's history, the arrival and influence of the Celts represent a pivotal thread woven into the fabric of the island's cultural evolution. The Celtic peoples, renowned for their vibrant art, rich oral traditions, and distinctive way of life, left an indelible mark on Ireland's landscape and identity.

The Celts, a diverse group of Indo-European tribes, are believed to have begun their migration across Europe around 1200 BCE. These migrations brought Celtic peoples to various regions, including the Iberian Peninsula, Central Europe, and the British Isles, including Ireland. By the time they reached the island, around 300 BCE, they encountered the existing inhabitants, contributing to the complex tapestry of Ireland's population.

The Celtic influence manifested itself in numerous aspects of Irish society, starting with language. Old Irish, a Goidelic Celtic language, emerged as the predominant tongue, fostering a sense of shared identity among the inhabitants. The Brehon Laws, an intricate legal system devised by the Celts, regulated aspects of daily life, reflecting their organized governance.

Artistry flourished under Celtic hands. Intricate metalwork, characterized by designs such as spirals, knots, and animals, showcased their craftsmanship and aesthetic sensibilities. The Ardagh Chalice and the Tara Brooch are masterpieces that have survived through the ages, captivating modern admirers with their intricate beauty.

The Celts also brought their spiritual beliefs to the island. The pantheon of gods and goddesses they worshiped found echoes in the mythological landscape of Ireland, intertwining with the island's own ancient legends. The Celts' reverence for nature was reflected in their sacred sites, such as hillforts, stone circles, and burial mounds.

Perhaps the most iconic Celtic contribution was their oral tradition. Bards and druids were the custodians of this rich heritage, passing down stories, poetry, and histories through generations. These oral traditions, interwoven with myth, provided a sense of continuity and community, enabling the transmission of cultural values and collective memory.

The Celtic tribes were not a monolithic entity; rather, they comprised diverse groups with distinct regional identities. In Ireland, these groups evolved into the various kingdoms and territories that would shape the island's political landscape. Tribes like the Ulaid in Ulster, the Laighin in Leinster, the Connachta in Connacht, and the Muma in Munster formed the foundation of the island's geopolitical organization.

Celtic influence, however, did not remain isolated to Ireland. Interactions with other Celtic peoples, as well as with Roman and later Christian cultures, created a complex web of cross-cultural exchange. The arrival of Christianity in Ireland, most notably attributed to St. Patrick, transformed Celtic spirituality, intertwining it with the new faith and further shaping the island's cultural identity.

In tracing the arrival and influence of the Celts, we delve into a chapter of Ireland's history characterized by diversity, creativity, and interconnectedness. The Celts brought with them a vibrant legacy that resonates in the language, art, spirituality, and governance of the island. As we continue our exploration, we will uncover how these threads of Celtic heritage intertwined with subsequent chapters of Ireland's history, leaving a legacy that endures in the hearts and minds of its people.

Fabled Tuatha Dé Danann: Myths, Legends, and Ancient Beliefs

In the enchanting tapestry of Ireland's ancient past, the legends of the Tuatha Dé Danann stand as luminous threads woven with magic, mystery, and a profound connection to the spiritual realm. These mythical beings, often referred to as "The People of the Goddess Danu," emerge from the mists of Irish folklore as an essential part of the island's cultural heritage.

The Tuatha Dé Danann are enshrined in the Lebor Gabála Érenn, the "Book of Invasions," which chronicles the waves of mythical and historical settlers that shaped Ireland's destiny. According to this epic narrative, the Tuatha Dé Danann arrived in Ireland by way of four great cities, bringing with them advanced skills in magic, craftsmanship, and healing.

Their arrival was not unopposed. The Tuatha Dé Danann clashed with the Fir Bolg, the earlier inhabitants of the land, in a series of epic battles that have become the stuff of legend. The most iconic of these conflicts was the Battle of Mag Tuired, a confrontation filled with magical feats and heroic deeds. In this battle, the Tuatha Dé Danann emerged victorious, claiming dominion over the land.

These mythical beings possessed extraordinary powers and knowledge. Brigid, for instance, represented both the goddess of poetry and healing, embodying the intertwined nature of these arts in ancient Celtic society. Lugh, the god of light, skill, and crafts, showcased the reverence given to skills and innovation. The Tuatha Dé Danann also maintained a connection with the land's mystical landscapes. The Sidhe, often referred to as "fairy mounds," were said to be portals to their realm. These hidden entrances were believed to be scattered across the Irish countryside, leading to the Otherworld, a realm of beauty and enchantment parallel to our own.

The intertwining of the Tuatha Dé Danann's mythical world with the fabric of everyday life is reflected in the practices of ancient Celtic spirituality. Rituals, sacrifices, and gatherings were held in honor of these deities, seeking their favor and protection. The cycles of nature, such as the solstices and equinoxes, were celebrated as sacred moments of connection between the mortal realm and the divine.

As Christianity spread across Ireland, the legacy of the Tuatha Dé Danann found a unique synthesis with the new faith. Many of the deities were reimagined as saints or merged with Christian figures, allowing for a seamless transition from ancient beliefs to the emerging religious framework. This fusion is evident in the reverence for sites that were sacred to both the ancient gods and the Christian saints.

In delving into the myths, legends, and ancient beliefs of the Tuatha Dé Danann, we encounter a world where the boundaries between the mortal and the mystical are blurred. Their stories reflect a profound reverence for nature, a celebration of human creativity, and a recognition of the sacred in the everyday. These tales continue to resonate in Ireland's cultural identity, inviting us to explore the complex tapestry of beliefs that have shaped the island's spiritual landscape.

High Kings and Tribal Realms: The Rise of Gaelic Power

As the mists of time gradually lifted over Ireland's landscape, a new chapter in its history emerged: the era of high kings and tribal realms. This period, characterized by a delicate balance between local chieftains and overarching rulers, saw the gradual consolidation of Gaelic power and the establishment of dynastic authority that left an indelible mark on the island's destiny.

The foundation of Gaelic society rested on the concept of tribalism, where distinct clans or septs held sway over specific territories. These tribal realms, known as túatha, formed the building blocks of Gaelic governance. Each túath was governed by a chieftain, known as a rí, who held both political and military authority within their domain.

Among these rí, a system of overkingship emerged. The high king, or ard rí, wielded authority over multiple túatha and chieftains, overseeing the broader political landscape. This hierarchical structure sought to strike a balance between unity and regional autonomy, allowing local chieftains to exercise control over their lands while acknowledging the overarching authority of the high king.

The Hill of Tara, located in County Meath, played a central role in this system of high kingship. Tara served as the symbolic heart of Gaelic political power, where high kings were inaugurated through ritualistic ceremonies. The Lia Fáil, the Stone of Destiny, was said to roar when the rightful high king ascended the throne, solidifying the ruler's legitimacy in the eyes of the people. The rise of Gaelic power was often punctuated by power struggles, alliances, and conflicts. The Clann Cholmáin, the Uí Néill, and the Érainn were prominent dynasties that vied for supremacy. The Connachta, hailing from Connacht, produced legendary figures like Queen Medb and King Ailill, whose exploits are immortalized in the Ulster Cycle of Irish mythology.

The Battle of Clontarf in 1014 is a pivotal event that encapsulates this era's dynamics. Brian Boru, the high king of Ireland, led an alliance of tribes against Viking invaders and their allies. The battle ended with Brian's victory but also claimed his life, marking a turning point in the relationship between Gaelic tribes and Viking settlements. The Brehon Laws, a complex legal system rooted in ancient traditions, governed Gaelic society during this period. These laws delineated rights, responsibilities, and penalties, emphasizing the importance of kinship, property rights, and restitution. The Brehon Laws showcased the intricate balance between centralized authority and local autonomy.

Despite the veneer of unity, the era of high kings and tribal realms was marked by internal divisions and external pressures. The arrival of Norman invaders in the 12th century introduced new challenges, altering the political landscape and shaping Ireland's path for centuries to come.

The rise of Gaelic power during this era painted a portrait of a society navigating the delicate dance between regional autonomy and overarching authority. The dynamic interplay between high kings and tribal chieftains is a testament to the complexity of early Gaelic governance, offering a window into the intricate tapestry of Ireland's political evolution.

Vikings on Irish Shores: Raids, Settlements, and Cultural Exchange

In the annals of Ireland's history, the arrival of the Vikings marked a dramatic shift in the island's trajectory, introducing waves of raids, settlements, and a complex web of cultural exchange. These seafaring warriors, hailing from the Scandinavian lands, left an indelible imprint on Ireland's society, shaping its political landscape, trade networks, and cultural identity.

The Viking Age, spanning roughly from the late 8th century to the mid-11th century, witnessed the emergence of Norse raiders on Irish shores. These raiders, driven by a desire for wealth and adventure, carried out swift and devastating attacks on coastal monasteries, towns, and settlements. These raids, while often brutal, were instrumental in reshaping Ireland's political dynamics by challenging existing power structures.

One of the most infamous Viking raids occurred in 795 when the Vikings pillaged the monastery at Rathlin Island. This marked the beginning of a period of turmoil as Viking longships, with their fearsome dragon heads, navigated Ireland's waterways, leaving a trail of destruction in their wake. Notable targets included the monastic settlements of Iona and Lindisfarne, showcasing the vulnerability of these spiritual centers.

However, the Vikings' impact on Ireland wasn't solely marked by violence. As the raids intensified, some Norse warriors established more permanent settlements along the coast. Dublin, in particular, evolved from a Viking encampment into a bustling trading hub known as Dyflin. The establishment of trading posts like Dublin and Waterford allowed for the exchange of goods, cultures, and ideas between the Norse and the native Irish.

The Vikings' influence extended beyond the realm of conflict and commerce. As these Scandinavian settlers intermingled with the local population, elements of Norse culture began to meld with Irish traditions. This fusion was evident in art, where motifs like serpent imagery and interlace patterns found their way into Irish manuscripts and metalwork. Even the Irish language absorbed Norse words, enriching its lexicon.

The establishment of Norse-Gaelic dynasties, such as the Uí Ímair, marked the blurring of cultural boundaries. These dynasties often held sway over both Norse and Gaelic territories, showcasing the fluidity of political allegiance during this era. The Viking influence reached its zenith with the reign of Brian Boru, who managed to unify many of these factions and repel Viking forces at the Battle of Clontarf in 1014.

The Vikings' presence on Irish shores also left a legacy in place names, where cities and landmarks still bear the Norse influence today. Beyond that, artifacts excavated from Viking settlements and burial sites provide a tangible connection to this pivotal period, offering a glimpse into the daily lives of these seafaring people.

In exploring the Vikings' impact on Ireland, we encounter a chapter characterized by both conflict and collaboration. The raiders' ferocity disrupted the existing order, while their settlements and interactions left an indelible mark on

Ireland's culture and heritage. The Vikings' legacy serves as a reminder that history is a tapestry woven with threads of conquest and connection, shaping the mosaic that is Ireland's rich and diverse identity.

Medieval Monasteries: Preserving Knowledge in a Time of Turmoil

In the heart of medieval Ireland, amidst the ebb and flow of power struggles and societal shifts, stood a bastion of stability and enlightenment: the monasteries. These religious sanctuaries, adorned with intricate architecture and nestled within idyllic landscapes, served as beacons of knowledge, faith, and cultural preservation during an era characterized by turmoil and uncertainty.

The monastic movement gained significant traction during the early medieval period, catalyzed by the spread of Christianity across the island. The first known monastery, established by St. Patrick himself, laid the foundation for a network of spiritual and intellectual centers that would shape Ireland's destiny for centuries to come.

These monasteries, often situated in remote and tranquil locales, became sanctuaries for those seeking solace from the chaos of the outside world. In this haven of contemplation, monks embraced a life of prayer, study, and devotion. The ideals of humility, piety, and community guided their daily existence, fostering a sense of shared purpose.

One of the most iconic symbols of these monastic communities is the round tower. These tall, cylindrical structures, often found near monastic sites, served as watchtowers, bell towers, and repositories for precious manuscripts and artifacts. Their distinctive design also held symbolic significance, representing the connection between the earthly realm and the divine.

The monks within these monasteries were not only spiritual devotees but also custodians of knowledge. In a time when literacy was a rarity, the monastic scriptoria played a crucial role in the preservation and creation of manuscripts. Illuminated manuscripts, adorned with intricate illustrations and embellishments, showcased the monks' dedication to preserving ancient texts, religious scriptures, and even secular knowledge.

Perhaps the most renowned of these manuscripts is the Book of Kells, a masterpiece of artistry and craftsmanship. Its intricate designs, richly adorned pages, and intricate calligraphy stand as a testament to the monks' commitment to their craft. The Book of Kells and other manuscripts like the Book of Durrow and the Lindisfarne Gospels serve as windows into a world where faith, art, and learning converged.

These monastic communities also played a role in education. The establishment of scriptoria fostered an environment of learning where monks and students copied and transcribed texts, ensuring the transmission of knowledge across generations. Monastic schools attracted scholars from across Europe, contributing to Ireland's reputation as a center of learning.

The preservation of classical knowledge and the transmission of Christianity were closely intertwined in these monasteries. Latin, the language of the Church, was the medium of instruction and communication. Monks diligently copied not only religious texts but also works of philosophy, science, and literature from the classical world, thereby preserving valuable insights for future generations.

In an era marked by political upheaval, Viking raids, and external pressures, the monasteries remained steadfast. They not only preserved knowledge but also acted as centers of refuge and solace. Their influence extended beyond Ireland, as scholars and manuscripts from Irish monasteries traveled across Europe, enriching the continent's intellectual and cultural landscape.

The story of medieval monasteries in Ireland is one of resilience, dedication, and the timeless pursuit of knowledge. These sanctuaries stood as bulwarks against the tides of uncertainty, preserving the legacy of the past while sowing the seeds of the future. Their legacy endures in the manuscripts, art, and architectural marvels that grace the Irish landscape and continue to inspire generations with their enduring wisdom.

Bards and Poets: Literature as the Soul of Medieval Ireland

In the midst of Ireland's medieval tapestry, where monasteries and castles stood as pillars of society, another vibrant facet emerged: the bards and poets. These gifted wordsmiths, weaving stories, songs, and verses with eloquence and passion, breathed life into Ireland's cultural identity, nurturing a literary tradition that resonates to this day.

The bards and poets of medieval Ireland were not mere entertainers; they held a revered and essential role within Gaelic society. Their words were the threads that wove together the fabric of the community, preserving history, myth, and societal values through the medium of oral tradition. The spoken word was their art, their craft, and their sacred duty.

The poetic tradition was governed by a complex set of rules and conventions. Bards were expected to memorize vast amounts of genealogy, history, and legend, making them repositories of cultural memory. Their training was rigorous and multifaceted, encompassing language, meter, mythology, and rhetoric. The three primary classes of poets were the fili (scholars and historians), the bard (songwriters and storytellers), and the seanachaidh (genealogists and lorekeepers).

Their poems and songs were diverse, ranging from elegies to epic tales, from satirical verses to odes praising kings and warriors. They composed laments that mourned the fallen and celebrated heroes, bridging the gap between the living and the ancestors. The poet's role in shaping and reflecting the collective consciousness of the community was both vital and profound.

The bardic tradition thrived within the courts of kings and chieftains. Bards were patrons of their craft, providing not only shelter and sustenance but also the honor and recognition befitting their artistic contributions. The courtly environment fostered a sense of competition and camaraderie among poets, driving them to excel in their craft.

The fluidity of the oral tradition meant that the bards and poets were instrumental in the dissemination of history, myth, and cultural values. Tales of heroic deeds, legendary figures like Cú Chulainn and Fionn mac Cumhaill, and the exploits of the Tuatha Dé Danann were carried from one generation to the next through their skilled recitations. This oral transmission ensured the continuity of Ireland's cultural heritage even in the absence of written records.

The decline of Gaelic power and the influence of the English language posed challenges to the bardic tradition. Nonetheless, the spirit of the poets endured. Their role transformed from courtly patronage to the expression of national identity and resistance. Poets like Aodhagán Ó Rathaille and Eoghan Rua Ó Súilleabháin used their verses to capture the resilience of the Gaelic people and the yearning for cultural preservation.

The bardic tradition's influence extended beyond the borders of Ireland. Its legacy can be felt in the poetic form known as "Aisling," where Ireland herself was personified as a beautiful woman visited in dreams, lamenting the nation's state and calling for its renewal. This metaphorical approach resonated with poets across Europe, leaving an imprint on the continent's literary landscape.

In exploring the role of bards and poets as the soul of medieval Ireland, we encounter a testament to the power of language, memory, and artistry. Their words bridged the gap between past and present, instilling a sense of continuity and identity within a society marked by change. The legacy of these literary luminaries illuminates the pages of history, serving as a reminder of the enduring power of storytelling and the human impulse to express the ineffable through the beauty of words.

Norman Conquests: Shaping a New Order on Irish Soil

In the medieval tapestry of Ireland's history, a new thread emerged with the arrival of the Normans. This chapter, marked by conquest, colonization, and the forging of new alliances, ushered in a period of transformation that left an indelible mark on the island's political landscape and cultural identity.

The Norman influence was catalyzed by the events of 1066, when William the Conqueror's victory at the Battle of Hastings in England sent ripples across Europe. The Normans, originally descendants of Vikings who settled in what is now Normandy, France, established a powerful presence in England and Wales. Their eyes soon turned toward Ireland, a land rich with potential for conquest and expansion.

The first significant Norman incursions occurred in the late 12th century. Strongbow, Richard de Clare, responded to an Irish invitation for aid, setting the stage for a series of Norman conquests. The marriage of Strongbow to the daughter of Dermot MacMurrough, the ousted King of Leinster, solidified this alliance and granted Strongbow a claim to the throne.

The Norman presence intensified with the arrival of King Henry II in 1171. His establishment of a royal administration marked the beginning of a period of colonization and territorial expansion. The Anglo-Normans introduced feudalism, castles, and a centralized legal system to Ireland. The influx of settlers from England and Wales established "Lordships" that stretched from the eastern coast to the interior.

This period was marked by conflict as the Normans sought to consolidate their control over Irish territories. The Gaelic lords, once mighty rulers in their own right, now faced the challenge of adapting to the Norman presence. The dynamic of power struggles and alliances reshaped the political landscape, often blurring the lines between Gaelic and Norman identities.

The impact of the Normans extended beyond political conquest. The architectural legacy of their presence is visible in the many castles and fortifications that dot the Irish countryside. Trim Castle, Carrickfergus Castle, and others stand as formidable reminders of their military prowess and architectural innovation. These structures marked a departure from the previous round tower design, showcasing the Normans' distinct architectural style.

Norman influence also shaped Ireland's legal and administrative systems. The introduction of the "Lordship of Ireland" established a central authority overseeing land tenure, taxation, and legal matters. This system led to the creation of English-style towns and the emergence of urban centers as trade and commerce thrived.

As the centuries progressed, the cultural and political lines between the Normans and the native Irish began to blur. Intermarriage, cultural exchange, and the merging of languages led to a gradual integration of the two communities. The Gaelic nobility adopted Norman practices, including surnames, heraldry, and land ownership patterns.

The Norman era laid the groundwork for the complex relationship between England and Ireland that would continue for centuries. The Normans' legacy is visible in the surnames, place names, and architectural landmarks that dot the landscape. It also serves as a reminder of the intricate interplay between conquest, assimilation, and the forging of new identities.

In delving into the Norman conquests and their impact on Ireland, we uncover a chapter that encapsulates the tensions and transformations that shaped the island's history. This era's echoes can still be heard in Ireland's modern landscape, a testament to the enduring legacy of a period that reshaped the political and cultural contours of the Emerald Isle.

Plantations and Struggles: Tudor and Stuart Influences

Amidst the winds of change that swept across Europe, the Tudor and Stuart influences on Ireland marked a chapter defined by plantations, power struggles, and cultural clashes. This period, spanning the 16th and 17th centuries, laid the foundation for enduring tensions between England and Ireland, leaving a lasting impact on both the political landscape and the fabric of Irish society.

The Tudor dynasty's reign marked a significant shift in Ireland's relationship with England. The Crown's desire for control, security, and religious uniformity led to a policy of colonization and plantation. The Tudor rulers sought to displace the native Irish and replace them with English and Scottish settlers who would conform to Protestantism.

The plantation policy, most notably in Ulster, witnessed the seizure of land from Gaelic lords and their redistribution to English and Scottish settlers. The Ulster Plantation, initiated by James I, aimed to solidify English control by creating a loyal Protestant population. The settlers, known as "planters," brought with them their own customs, culture, and religious beliefs. These plantations, while intended to assert control, resulted in a complex landscape of ethnic, religious, and cultural diversity. The native Irish population often found themselves marginalized and dispossessed, fueling grievances that would simmer for generations. The Catholic faith, central to Irish identity, became a symbol of resistance against English rule. Religious strife further deepened the divide during the

Stuart era. The ascendancy of James II, a Catholic monarch, stirred fears among Protestant elites who saw their power and privileges threatened. The Protestant majority in Ireland, particularly in Ulster, became staunch defenders of their faith and political influence, setting the stage for religious and political conflict.

The period was marked by a series of uprisings and rebellions. The Nine Years' War, waged from 1594 to 1603, saw Hugh O'Neill and his allies challenge English rule. The defeat of the Gaelic lords marked the end of the native Irish aristocracy's power, solidifying English dominance. The impact of these struggles was evident in the socio-economic fabric of Irish society. The Penal Laws, enacted by the English Crown to suppress Catholicism, marginalized the Catholic population. These laws restricted land ownership, political participation, and educational opportunities for Catholics, effectively marginalizing them within their own homeland.

The Battle of the Boyne in 1690, a pivotal conflict during the Williamite War, cemented the Protestant ascendancy and further entrenched divisions. The victory of William of Orange over James II bolstered Protestant rule and set the stage for centuries of sectarian tension.

In exploring the Tudor and Stuart influences on Ireland, we delve into a period where colonization, religious strife, and power struggles intersected to shape a complex socio-political landscape. This era laid the groundwork for the divisions that would endure for generations, as the threads of history intertwined to create a narrative marked by resilience, resistance, and a pursuit of identity in the face of adversity.

Cromwell's Shadow: The Impact of the English Civil Wars

The 17th century brought forth a tumultuous period that reverberated far beyond the borders of England: the English Civil Wars. Amidst the clash of ideologies, royalist loyalty, and parliamentary aspirations, Ireland found itself entangled in a web of conflict that left an enduring impact, forever shaping its political, social, and cultural landscape.

The catalyst for this turmoil was the power struggle between King Charles I and the English Parliament. The refusal to grant the king absolute authority led to a series of conflicts that culminated in the outbreak of the English Civil War in 1642. The conflict pitted the Royalists, who supported the monarchy, against the Parliamentarians, who sought greater political influence.

In Ireland, the Civil Wars held a unique resonance. The predominantly Catholic population held mixed allegiances. While some supported the king and his cause, others saw an opportunity to challenge the Protestant Ascendancy and English rule. The divisions within Irish society mirrored those unfolding in England, adding a layer of complexity to the conflict.

Oliver Cromwell, a pivotal figure in English history, cast a shadow that stretched across Ireland during this period. His leadership of the New Model Army and his subsequent conquest of Ireland had a profound impact. Cromwell's military campaigns were marked by brutality, particularly in the siege of Drogheda and Wexford, where massacres occurred. His goal was to crush Irish resistance and assert English control.

The Cromwellian Conquest of Ireland, which unfolded from 1649 to 1653, led to a massive redistribution of land. Catholic landowners who had supported the Royalists saw their estates confiscated and redistributed to Cromwell's soldiers and English settlers. This marked a significant blow to the Catholic population's economic and political power.

Cromwell's impact extended beyond land confiscations. The Cromwellian Settlement also included the transplantation of Irish Catholics to Connacht, further displacing populations and fostering bitterness. These policies aimed to solidify Protestant control and minimize the potential for future rebellion.

The Restoration of Charles II in 1660 saw the monarchy reinstated, but the repercussions of Cromwell's actions lingered. The Test Act of 1673, which required public officeholders to renounce Catholicism, reinforced divisions and discrimination. The legacy of Cromwell's reign loomed large, shaping the relationship between England and Ireland for generations.

Cultural and social scars also endured. The Irish language and Catholic faith suffered suppression, and the scars of the brutal conflict left a lasting impact on collective memory. These experiences were reflected in literature, folk traditions, and oral histories, serving as a reminder of the resilience and perseverance of the Irish people.

In delving into the impact of the English Civil Wars on Ireland, we encounter a chapter of history that epitomizes the complexities of power, loyalty, and identity. The tumultuous events of this period left an indelible mark, shaping the trajectory of Ireland's evolution as a nation. The shadows cast by Cromwell's legacy continue to resonate, a testament to the enduring impact of historical forces on the cultural and political contours of a land and its people.

Era of Revolution: From the United Irishmen to the Act of Union

The late 18th and early 19th centuries witnessed an era of profound change in Ireland's history, marked by the rise of revolutionary movements, calls for reform, and the tumultuous journey towards the Act of Union. This chapter encapsulates a period of upheaval, aspirations, and political maneuvering that would shape the course of Irish history for centuries to come.

The seeds of revolution were sown by the United Irishmen, a movement born out of a desire for political and religious equality, independence, and representation. Formed in the 1790s, the United Irishmen sought to bridge religious and sectarian divides, advocating for a united Ireland free from English rule. Their aspirations resonated across religious lines, as Catholics and Protestants alike rallied behind the cause.

The United Irishmen's ideals found expression in the 1798 Rebellion, a pivotal moment in Irish history. The rebellion, marked by armed uprisings and clashes with British forces, aimed to establish an independent Irish republic. However, the rebellion was brutally suppressed, leading to a heavy loss of life and the defeat of the revolutionary forces.

The aftermath of the rebellion saw a tightening of English control and a crackdown on Irish dissent. The Act of Union, passed in 1800, marked a turning point. The act aimed to unite Ireland and Great Britain under a single political entity, dissolving the Irish Parliament and incorporating Irish representatives into the British Parliament. This move was met with opposition, as many saw it as a loss of Irish sovereignty and a betrayal of the United Irishmen's ideals.

The Act of Union was met with resistance and protests. Prominent figures like Robert Emmet and Daniel O'Connell continued to advocate for Irish rights and autonomy. O'Connell's efforts in the early 19th century centered on the Catholic Emancipation movement, which sought to end religious discrimination against Catholics and allow them to hold public office.

The Great Famine of the mid-19th century further highlighted the injustices faced by the Irish population. The famine, caused by a potato blight, led to widespread death, suffering, and emigration. The lack of effective British response to the crisis intensified feelings of resentment and alienation.

The era of revolution and reform also saw cultural and literary movements that celebrated Irish identity. The Gaelic Revival, characterized by a resurgence of interest in Irish language, literature, and traditions, aimed to reclaim and preserve Irish cultural heritage. Figures like W.B. Yeats and Lady Gregory played a pivotal role in this movement, fostering a sense of national pride and identity.

As the 19th century progressed, political landscapes shifted. The Home Rule movement, championed by leaders like Charles Stewart Parnell, aimed to secure a level of self-governance for Ireland within the British Empire. The movement garnered significant support but also faced staunch opposition from those who feared Irish autonomy.

The journey from the United Irishmen to the Act of Union was one of struggle, aspirations, and evolving ideologies. The voices of revolutionaries, reformers, and cultural pioneers left an indelible mark on Ireland's identity. The echoes of this era continue to resonate in the fabric of Irish society, shaping the ongoing quest for self-determination and the exploration of what it means to be Irish in a rapidly changing world.

Great Famine: A Nation's Tragic Ordeal and Diaspora

The Great Famine, an indelible chapter in Irish history, stands as a tragic testament to the convergence of factors that can lead to immense human suffering. This period, spanning from the mid-1840s to the early 1850s, saw Ireland engulfed in a devastating potato blight that caused widespread death, suffering, and a profound impact on the nation's demographics, culture, and identity.

The Irish population had become heavily reliant on the potato as a staple crop, particularly among the rural poor. The potato blight, Phytophthora infestans, struck with unprecedented ferocity in 1845, causing the potato crops to rot in the ground. The subsequent years saw continued blight, causing successive crop failures and leading to a catastrophic food shortage.

The impact of the potato blight was compounded by a complex set of social, economic, and political factors. Ireland was under British rule, and a combination of absentee landlords, unequal land distribution, and limited land reform meant that many Irish peasants were impoverished and had little access to other food sources. The lack of a comprehensive relief effort from the British government exacerbated the crisis.

The scale of the suffering during the Great Famine was immense. Crop failures led to widespread hunger, malnutrition, and diseases. The population's vulnerability was further heightened by poor living conditions and lack of access to basic healthcare. Mass emigration was driven by desperation, as people sought to escape the horrors of the famine and the bleak future it promised.

The famine's impact was particularly acute on the rural population. Entire families were devastated by hunger and disease, leading to high mortality rates. The heart-wrenching stories of families forced to leave their homes in search of food and relief are etched into the collective memory of Ireland.

The famine had far-reaching effects on Irish society, culture, and demographics. The death toll is estimated to be between one million and 1.5 million people, with millions more emigrating to escape the dire circumstances. The Irish population, which had been steadily growing, saw a steep decline, leaving a lasting demographic impact that is still felt today.

Emigration became a lifeline for many Irish families. The Irish diaspora spread to countries like the United States, Canada, Australia, and beyond. Irish immigrants faced hardship and discrimination in their new homes, but they also contributed significantly to the societies they joined, leaving an enduring impact on global culture, politics, and economy.

The Great Famine also had a profound impact on Irish identity and cultural memory. The trauma and loss experienced during this period left a mark on the nation's psyche. The famine became a touchstone for understanding the resilience and solidarity of the Irish people in the face of adversity.

The echoes of the Great Famine reverberate in modern Ireland. The tragedy serves as a reminder of the importance of social and economic justice, as well as the need for solidarity in times of crisis. The scars of the famine are etched into the landscape and memory of the nation, honoring the memory of those who suffered while inspiring a collective commitment to ensuring that such a tragedy is never repeated.

Home Rule Dreams: Political Agitation and Calls for Autonomy

In the latter half of the 19th century, a new chapter of Irish history unfolded, characterized by fervent political activism, aspirations for autonomy, and the pursuit of self-governance. This era saw the emergence of the Home Rule movement, which sought to secure a level of self-government for Ireland within the British Empire. The echoes of this movement reverberate through the annals of Irish history, marking a crucial step in the nation's journey towards autonomy.

The call for Home Rule was born out of the desire for Irish representation and the right to govern domestic affairs. The movement gained momentum in the wake of the Act of Union of 1800, which had united the Irish and British Parliaments. The lack of Irish self-governance and the dominance of English interests in the Irish Parliament fueled grievances that spanned religious, political, and social divides.

The leader at the forefront of the Home Rule movement was Charles Stewart Parnell. Parnell's charismatic leadership and strategic prowess galvanized support across Irish society. He formed the Irish Parliamentary Party and, through disciplined parliamentary tactics, managed to secure concessions from the British government that brought the question of Irish self-governance to the forefront of political discourse.

The Home Rule movement was characterized by a sense of unity that transcended religious affiliations. Catholics and Protestants alike saw Home Rule as a means to attain political representation and cultural preservation. This sense of shared aspiration was epitomized by the famous phrase "Catholic, Protestant, and Dissenter," underscoring the movement's inclusive nature.

Despite the support it garnered, the Home Rule movement faced staunch opposition, particularly from Unionist forces in Ireland's northern province of Ulster. These Unionists, predominantly Protestant, feared that Home Rule would result in their political and cultural marginalization within an overwhelmingly Catholic Irish state. The resistance of Unionists laid the foundation for a deep-seated division that would shape Irish politics for decades.

The Home Rule Bill of 1886 marked a significant milestone in the movement. While the bill ultimately failed to pass, it brought the question of Irish self-governance to the forefront of British politics. A second Home Rule Bill in 1893 encountered similar challenges, ultimately failing to receive royal assent.

The outbreak of World War I in 1914 disrupted the trajectory of the Home Rule movement. The third Home Rule Bill was set to become law, but the war's onset led to its suspension. The Ulster Covenant, signed by over 400,000 Unionists in 1912, expressed strong opposition to Home Rule in Ulster and heightened political tensions.

The turbulent period that followed saw the rise of paramilitary groups on both sides of the Home Rule debate. The establishment of the Ulster Volunteer Force (UVF) and the Irish Volunteers reflected the growing polarization and the potential for violence. The outbreak of World War I temporarily shelved the Home Rule question as both nationalist and Unionist forces enlisted in the war effort.

The events of the Easter Rising in 1916, followed by the subsequent struggle for independence, would reshape the trajectory of Ireland's political landscape. The legacy of the Home Rule movement, while not leading directly to the establishment of a self-governing Irish state, laid the groundwork for the broader quest for independence and self-determination.

The era of Home Rule dreams and political agitation underscores the importance of political mobilization and the enduring pursuit of autonomy. The movement's legacy is woven into the fabric of Ireland's identity, inspiring generations to stand up for their rights and to forge a path towards a future defined by self-governance, unity, and shared aspirations.

Easter Rising: Pivotal Moments in Ireland's Fight for Independence

The dawn of the 20th century ushered in a new era of resistance and determination in Ireland's quest for independence. At the heart of this era stood the Easter Rising of 1916, a pivotal moment that encapsulated the spirit of defiance, sacrifice, and the unyielding pursuit of national sovereignty.

The roots of the Easter Rising can be traced to the deep-seated desire for self-determination that had simmered throughout Ireland's history. The movement gained momentum as dissatisfaction with British rule grew, fueled by factors such as political marginalization, cultural suppression, and the legacy of struggles like the Home Rule movement.

The leaders of the Easter Rising were drawn from a cross-section of Irish society, reflecting the movement's inclusive nature. Figures like Patrick Pearse, James Connolly, and Joseph Plunkett emerged as key architects of the rebellion. Their ideologies varied, spanning from cultural nationalism to socialist ideals, but they shared a common goal: to strike a blow against British rule and proclaim an independent Irish Republic.

The Rising unfolded on Easter Monday, April 24, 1916, as Irish rebels seized key locations in Dublin. The General Post Office (GPO) became the epicenter of the rebellion, serving as the headquarters from which the Proclamation of the Irish Republic was read. The proclamation declared the establishment of an Irish Republic, asserting the right of the Irish people to self-governance and the ownership of Ireland's resources.

The Rising, however, faced significant challenges from the outset. The rebels were outnumbered and lacked sufficient support from the general population. A combination of poor planning, communication breakdowns, and limited weaponry hampered their efforts. The British response was swift and brutal, with British forces moving to suppress the rebellion.

The week-long conflict that ensued witnessed intense fighting and urban warfare in Dublin's streets. The rebels faced not only the might of the British military but also the skepticism of the Irish population. The destruction and civilian casualties that resulted from the clashes cast a shadow over the Rising's immediate aftermath.

The surrender of the rebels on April 29, 1916, marked a turning point. The leaders of the Rising were arrested and imprisoned, and British authorities sought to quell any remaining sentiment for rebellion. However, the heavy-handed response of the British government led to a shift in public opinion. The execution of 15 leaders, including Pearse and Connolly, galvanized sympathy for the cause and turned the rebels into martyrs.

The legacy of the Easter Rising reverberated far beyond its immediate aftermath. The Rising had captured the imagination of many and stirred the collective consciousness of the Irish population. The seeds of the rebellion had been sown, and the spirit of resistance continued to grow in the face of adversity.

The political landscape of Ireland shifted dramatically in the years following the Rising. The rise of Sinn Féin, a political party advocating for an independent Irish Republic, gained momentum. The 1918 general election marked a seismic shift, as Sinn Féin's victory saw them abstain from the British Parliament and establish their own parliament in Dublin, the first Dáil Éireann.

The events of the Easter Rising had set the stage for a protracted struggle for independence. The War of Independence, marked by guerrilla warfare and negotiations, would ultimately lead to the Anglo-Irish Treaty of 1921 and the establishment of the Irish Free State. The Rising had left an indelible mark, serving as a touchstone for the resilience, sacrifice, and unity that would define Ireland's path towards nationhood.

War of Independence: From Guerrilla Warfare to Anglo-Irish Treaty

The aftermath of the Easter Rising set the stage for a new phase in Ireland's quest for independence—the War of Independence. This chapter delves into the period from 1919 to 1921, marked by guerrilla warfare, political negotiations, and the eventual signing of the Anglo-Irish Treaty that would pave the way for the establishment of the Irish Free State.

The War of Independence unfolded against a backdrop of mounting tensions between the Irish population and British forces. The harsh response to the Easter Rising, coupled with the enduring desire for self-determination, created an environment ripe for armed resistance. The conflict was characterized by irregular warfare, as Irish republicans employed guerrilla tactics against British military and police forces.

The Irish Republican Army (IRA) emerged as a central force in the War of Independence. Comprising fighters from a range of backgrounds and motivated by a shared goal of achieving an independent Irish republic, the IRA carried out ambushes, raids, and acts of sabotage. Michael Collins, a charismatic leader and strategist, played a pivotal role in shaping the IRA's approach to the conflict.

The war was marked by a series of high-profile incidents that garnered international attention. The Soloheadbeg ambush in January 1919 is often considered the catalyst for the war, as it marked the first armed action by the IRA against British forces. The conflict escalated as ambushes, attacks, and reprisals became increasingly common.

The British response to the guerrilla warfare was marked by a cycle of violence and counter-violence. The "Black and Tans," a paramilitary force composed of British World War I veterans, were notorious for their brutality and reprisal tactics. The violence of the war left scars on both sides, with civilian populations caught in the crossfire.

The political landscape was shifting as well. Sinn Féin, which had gained significant support in the wake of the Easter Rising, established Dáil Éireann—the Irish parliament—in 1919. The Dáil's Declaration of Independence asserted Ireland's right to self-governance and rejected British authority. The dual track of political and military resistance demonstrated the unity of purpose among Irish republicans.

Negotiations between the British government and Irish representatives began in earnest in 1921. The Anglo-Irish Treaty, signed on December 6, 1921, marked a pivotal moment. The treaty recognized the Irish Free State as a self-governing dominion within the British Commonwealth, granting Ireland a level of autonomy. However, the terms of the treaty, particularly the requirement to pledge allegiance to the British Crown, sparked intense debate and division among Irish republicans.

The signing of the Anglo-Irish Treaty was met with mixed reactions. While some saw it as a pragmatic step towards independence, others viewed it as a compromise that fell short of their aspirations. The split within the republican movement eventually culminated in the Irish Civil War, pitting pro-treaty forces against anti-treaty forces.

The War of Independence, despite its sacrifices and challenges, marked a significant step towards Ireland's nationhood. The conflict demonstrated the resilience, determination, and unity of the Irish people in the face of adversity. While the treaty and subsequent civil war created divisions, they also laid the groundwork for the establishment of the Irish Free State in 1922, marking a turning point in Ireland's journey towards self-governance and independence.

Civil War Chronicles: Divisions, Repercussions, and Reconciliation

The aftermath of the Anglo-Irish Treaty of 1921 set the stage for a bitter and tumultuous chapter in Irish history— the Irish Civil War. Spanning from 1922 to 1923, this conflict pitted former comrades-in-arms against each other, revealing the deep-seated divisions within the republican movement and leaving a lasting impact on Irish society, politics, and identity.

The seeds of the civil war were sown in the split over the Anglo-Irish Treaty itself. While the treaty had paved the way for the establishment of the Irish Free State, it also sparked intense disagreements among republicans over the question of allegiance to the British Crown. The pro-treaty faction believed that the treaty represented a pragmatic step towards achieving meaningful self-governance, while the anti-treaty faction deemed it a betrayal of the republican cause.

The civil war erupted in June 1922 when pro-treaty forces, loyal to the Free State government, moved against anti-treaty forces, who saw themselves as defenders of the original ideals of the Irish Republic. The conflict, marked by a series of battles, sieges, and reprisals, took a heavy toll on both sides. Former comrades and friends found themselves on opposing sides of the divide, leading to heart-wrenching confrontations.

The violence and bloodshed of the civil war left a mark on Irish society. Families were torn apart, and communities were divided. The war's impact was felt not only on the battlefield but also in the homes and hearts of the Irish people. The deep wounds inflicted during this period would continue to resonate for generations.

The civil war also had profound implications for the political landscape. The pro-treaty forces, led by Michael Collins, emerged victorious, securing control of the fledgling Free State. Collins' assassination in August 1922 was a blow to the pro-treaty side, but the momentum shifted in their favor. The anti-treaty forces, led by figures like Éamon de Valera, eventually surrendered in May 1923.

The conclusion of the civil war marked the beginning of a complex process of reconciliation and healing. The divisions that had torn Irish society apart needed to be addressed if the new nation was to move forward. The legacy of the civil war lingered, shaping political alliances and ideological divides for decades to come.

The civil war's impact extended to cultural and social spheres as well. Literature, art, and public discourse grappled with the questions of loyalty, sacrifice, and the complexities of nation-building. The scars of the conflict left a lasting imprint on the Irish psyche, influencing how the nation perceived itself and its place in the world.

Reconciliation was a gradual process that unfolded over time. Political leaders like de Valera sought to bridge the gaps between the pro-treaty and anti-treaty factions. The symbolic gesture of the Civil War Memorial, unveiled in Glasnevin Cemetery, aimed to honor all those who had sacrificed, regardless of which side they had fought for.

The aftermath of the civil war set the stage for the evolution of Irish politics. The rivalry between Fianna Fáil, founded by de Valera, and Fine Gael, the successor to the pro-treaty forces, became defining features of Irish political discourse. While divisions persisted, the lessons of the civil war also underscored the importance of unity and collaboration in shaping the nation's future.

In exploring the civil war chronicles, we encounter a chapter of history characterized by pain, sacrifice, and the complexities of nation-building. The conflict's legacy serves as a reminder of the challenges that arise when ideals clash and loyalties are divided. Yet, it also underscores the resilience of the Irish people in navigating the path towards reconciliation and the pursuit of a shared destiny.

Emerald Literature Revival: Literary Resurgence in a New Nation

As Ireland emerged from the tumultuous period of the early 20th century, a cultural renaissance took root, breathing new life into the nation's literary landscape. This chapter delves into the "Emerald Literature Revival," a period of artistic blossoming that spanned the early to mid-20th century, leaving an indelible mark on Irish literature and identity.

The revival of literature was closely intertwined with the broader quest for independence and self-determination. The cultural and political dimensions converged, as Irish writers sought to define and express a distinctive Irish identity in the wake of colonial rule and the establishment of the Irish Free State.

One of the key figures in this literary resurgence was W.B. Yeats, a poet, playwright, and founder of the Abbey Theatre. Yeats played a central role in the Celtic Revival, a movement that sought to revive and celebrate Ireland's Gaelic heritage. He drew inspiration from Irish mythology, folklore, and a sense of national pride, infusing his works with a distinctive Irish spirit.

The Abbey Theatre, founded in 1904, became a symbol of the literary revival. It provided a platform for Irish playwrights, actors, and directors to showcase their works, reflecting the aspirations and struggles of the Irish people. The plays presented at the Abbey often explored themes of

Irish history, identity, and the complexities of nation-building.

The literary revival was not confined to the theater alone. Poetry, fiction, and essay writing flourished as writers grappled with questions of Irishness, colonialism, and cultural heritage. Figures like Lady Gregory, J.M. Synge, and Padraic Pearse contributed to this literary renaissance, each bringing their unique perspectives and voices to the forefront.

The revival of the Irish language was also a central tenet of this movement. Efforts to revive and promote Irish as a spoken and written language gained momentum, driven by a desire to preserve a vital aspect of Irish culture and identity. The establishment of Conradh na Gaeilge (The Gaelic League) in 1893 played a crucial role in promoting the use of Irish language in everyday life.

The Easter Rising of 1916 further fueled the literary revival. The leaders of the Rising, particularly Patrick Pearse, were not only political activists but also poets and writers. Pearse's poetry, with its themes of sacrifice and nationhood, resonated deeply with the ideals of the time. The proclamation of the Irish Republic, read from the steps of the General Post Office during the Rising, became a powerful symbol of the intersection of literature and politics.

The legacy of the literary revival is enduring. The works produced during this period remain central to Irish literary canon. James Joyce's "Ulysses," published in 1922, stands as a seminal work of modernist literature, pushing the boundaries of narrative and language. The literature of this era explored the complexities of identity, the scars of history, and the journey towards self-discovery.

The Emerald Literature Revival not only left an indelible mark on Irish literature but also played a pivotal role in shaping the national consciousness. It provided a space for writers to explore the nuances of Irish identity, the challenges of nationhood, and the intricacies of cultural memory. This literary renaissance remains a testament to the enduring power of art to reflect, inspire, and unite a nation in its quest for self-expression and self-determination.

Partition and the North: The Complexities of Irish Division

The establishment of the Irish Free State in 1922 marked a significant milestone in Ireland's struggle for independence. However, it also left behind a legacy of division that would shape the course of Irish history for decades to come. This chapter explores the complexities of partition and the creation of Northern Ireland, delving into the social, political, and cultural dynamics that continue to define the region.

Partition, the division of Ireland into two separate entities, emerged as a solution to the political and religious tensions that had simmered for centuries. The Government of Ireland Act of 1920 led to the creation of Northern Ireland—a region predominantly composed of Protestant communities—while the rest of Ireland became the Irish Free State.

The partition of Ireland was deeply contentious and remains a topic of debate to this day. The boundaries drawn to demarcate Northern Ireland from the Irish Free State were not merely lines on a map; they reflected deep-seated divisions in religion, culture, and identity. The predominantly Protestant Unionist community in the north aligned itself with the United Kingdom, while the predominantly Catholic Nationalist community sought closer ties to the Irish Free State.

The religious and cultural schism was compounded by political factors. The Unionists in the north, fearing marginalization within an overwhelmingly Catholic Irish state, advocated for their own separate entity. The establishment of Northern Ireland was seen as a means of preserving their distinct identity and maintaining ties to the United Kingdom.

The early years of Northern Ireland were marked by tensions and conflicts. The Catholic minority in the region faced discrimination and marginalization, exacerbating existing divisions. The sectarian divide manifested in various ways, including unequal access to jobs, housing, and political representation.

The period from the 1960s onwards saw a surge in civil rights activism in Northern Ireland. The Catholic community, inspired by the broader global movements for equality, demanded an end to discriminatory practices. However, their efforts were met with resistance from Unionist authorities, leading to a spiral of violence and unrest.

The Troubles, a period of violent conflict that lasted from the late 1960s to the late 1990s, marked a dark chapter in Northern Ireland's history. The conflict pitted paramilitary groups, such as the Provisional Irish Republican Army (IRA), against British security forces and loyalist paramilitary organizations. The Troubles left a trail of death, destruction, and trauma, impacting communities on both sides of the divide.

Efforts to find a peaceful resolution to the conflict gained momentum in the late 20th century. The Good Friday Agreement of 1998, a landmark peace accord, aimed to address the political, social, and cultural grievances that had fueled the conflict. The agreement established a power-sharing government in Northern Ireland and laid the groundwork for ongoing reconciliation efforts.

The complexities of partition and its aftermath continue to shape the region's dynamics. The legacy of the Troubles, while gradually fading, still casts a shadow over Northern Ireland. The issues of identity, sovereignty, and unity remain central to the discussions surrounding the region's future.

In exploring the complexities of partition and the creation of Northern Ireland, we encounter a story defined by division, resilience, and the ongoing pursuit of peace. The dynamics that emerged from this period continue to inform the region's political landscape, highlighting the challenges and possibilities of building a shared future amidst diverse and sometimes conflicting aspirations.

The Troubles Unveiled: Decades of Conflict and Peace Efforts

The Troubles, a period of intense conflict and violence that engulfed Northern Ireland from the late 1960s to the late 1990s, left an indelible mark on the region's history, society, and psyche. This chapter delves into the complex chronicles of the Troubles, exploring the origins, dynamics, and the efforts towards peace that eventually emerged.

The origins of the Troubles can be traced back to the deep-seated divisions within Northern Ireland, stemming from historical, political, religious, and socio-economic factors. The Catholic Nationalist community sought closer ties with the Irish Free State and the Republic of Ireland, while the Protestant Unionist community identified strongly with the United Kingdom. These divisions were exacerbated by a history of discrimination, unequal access to opportunities, and unequal political representation.

The Troubles were characterized by a cycle of violence, with paramilitary groups on both sides engaging in acts of terrorism, bombings, assassinations, and ambushes. The Provisional Irish Republican Army (IRA), formed in 1969, sought to end British rule in Northern Ireland and establish a united Ireland. Loyalist paramilitary groups, such as the Ulster Volunteer Force (UVF), opposed this goal and sought to maintain Northern Ireland's ties to the UK.

The conflict had profound implications for Northern Ireland's society. Communities were torn apart, families were devastated by loss, and mistrust ran deep. Security checkpoints, curfews, and a heavy British military presence became part of daily life. The scars of the Troubles still linger in the physical landscape and the memories of those who lived through it.

Efforts to resolve the conflict and bring about peace were numerous and often complex. International involvement, particularly from the United States, played a significant role in facilitating negotiations. The Sunningdale Agreement of 1973 aimed to establish a power-sharing government in Northern Ireland, but it was short-lived due to Unionist opposition.

The hunger strikes in the early 1980s, led by IRA prisoners seeking political status, captured global attention and underscored the depth of the divisions. The Anglo-Irish Agreement of 1985, which involved cooperation between the British and Irish governments, sought to address some of the grievances but also faced criticism from Unionists.

The path to peace was arduous and marked by setbacks, but it ultimately led to the Good Friday Agreement of 1998. This historic accord aimed to address the key issues of governance, policing, decommissioning of weapons, and justice. The agreement paved the way for a power-sharing government and laid the groundwork for ongoing reconciliation efforts.

The signing of the Good Friday Agreement marked a turning point. Paramilitary groups on both sides gradually ceased their violent activities, and Northern Ireland experienced a period of relative calm. However, challenges remained, as the wounds of the Troubles were deep and reconciliation was a complex process.

The Troubles unveiled the complexity of Northern Ireland's divisions, the human cost of conflict, and the resilience of the people who lived through it. The period serves as a reminder of the importance of addressing grievances, promoting dialogue, and pursuing peaceful solutions to deeply entrenched conflicts. The ongoing efforts towards reconciliation and unity underscore the potential for a shared future, built upon the lessons of the past.

Cultural Renaissance: Art, Music, and Identity in Modern Ireland

As the 20th century unfolded, Ireland experienced a vibrant cultural renaissance that encompassed art, music, literature, and more. This chapter delves into the dynamic interplay of creativity, identity, and the modernization of Ireland's cultural landscape, highlighting the individuals and movements that shaped this period of artistic resurgence.

The cultural renaissance emerged as Ireland sought to define its identity in the aftermath of colonial rule and conflict. The pursuit of cultural expression was intimately linked with the broader quest for national self-determination. Artists and creators were driven by a desire to reclaim and celebrate Irish heritage while exploring new horizons that reflected the changing times.

Visual art played a significant role in this renaissance. The emergence of the Irish School of Landscape Painting in the late 19th and early 20th centuries paved the way for a unique artistic vision. Painters like Jack B. Yeats, Paul Henry, and Mainie Jellett captured the Irish landscape, imbuing their works with a sense of place and belonging. These artists were inspired by the natural beauty of Ireland's countryside, as well as its folklore and traditions.

Literature remained a powerful vehicle for cultural expression. The legacy of writers like W.B. Yeats, James Joyce, and Seamus Heaney continued to influence modern Irish literature. New generations of writers, poets, and playwrights emerged, exploring themes of identity, memory, and societal change. Authors like Edna O'Brien, John McGahern, and Roddy Doyle brought contemporary voices to the literary canon, grappling with the complexities of modern Irish life.

Music was another cornerstone of the cultural revival. Traditional Irish music experienced a resurgence, driven by a renewed interest in preserving and celebrating the country's musical heritage. Folk music, traditional ballads, and Irish dance became emblematic of the nation's identity. Artists like The Chieftains, Planxty, and Clannad blended traditional sounds with modern influences, captivating audiences both in Ireland and internationally.

Theatre and performance arts flourished during this period as well. The Abbey Theatre continued to showcase new plays that reflected the changing social and political landscape. Playwrights like Brian Friel, Marina Carr, and Martin McDonagh offered contemporary insights while building upon the legacy of their predecessors.

The resurgence of cultural expression was not without its challenges. The tension between tradition and modernity, rural and urban, and national and international influences shaped the discourse. Moreover, the question of language remained significant. Efforts to revive the Irish language gained momentum, with organizations like Conradh na Gaeilge (The Gaelic League) promoting Irish as a living language.

The late 20th century witnessed the global dissemination of Irish culture, partly due to the Irish diaspora and the influence of technology. St. Patrick's Day celebrations and Irish music festivals became iconic events worldwide. The music of U2, the success of Riverdance, and the cinematic achievements of directors like Neil Jordan and Jim Sheridan elevated Ireland's cultural profile on the global stage.

The cultural renaissance of modern Ireland continues to evolve. The blending of traditional and contemporary elements remains a hallmark of Irish creativity. Artists, musicians, and writers continue to explore the nuances of Irish identity, reflecting the ever-changing landscape of the nation and its place in the world. The legacy of this renaissance serves as a testament to the enduring power of culture to shape and illuminate the journey of a nation.

Celtic Tiger: Economic Transformation and Globalization

The term "Celtic Tiger" aptly encapsulates the remarkable economic transformation that Ireland underwent from the late 20th century into the early 21st century. This chapter delves into the factors that fueled this period of rapid growth, the challenges it posed, and the impact of globalization on Ireland's economy and society.

The origins of the Celtic Tiger can be traced back to the 1980s when Ireland embarked on a journey of economic liberalization and reform. The country shifted from protectionist policies to embracing free-market principles, attracting foreign direct investment and stimulating export-oriented industries. A skilled and educated workforce, coupled with Ireland's membership in the European Union (EU), provided a conducive environment for economic growth.

Foreign direct investment played a pivotal role in Ireland's economic resurgence. Multinational corporations, particularly in the technology, pharmaceutical, and finance sectors, established a significant presence in the country. The favorable corporate tax rate, coupled with the skilled workforce, made Ireland an attractive destination for companies seeking to expand their global operations.

One of the defining features of the Celtic Tiger era was the growth of the technology sector. The establishment of the International Financial Services Centre (IFSC) in Dublin further enhanced Ireland's status as a hub for global finance. Companies like Microsoft, Google, and Intel set up operations in Ireland, contributing to job creation, increased exports, and a surge in economic activity.

The construction and property sectors experienced a boom during the Celtic Tiger years. Rapid urbanization, coupled with a housing shortage, led to a surge in property prices and construction activity. However, this period also witnessed speculative practices and an unsustainable housing market, which would later contribute to economic challenges.

The impact of globalization was evident in various facets of Irish society. The increased interconnectedness of economies resulted in a surge in trade, tourism, and cultural exchange. The Irish diaspora, which had a strong presence in countries like the United States and the United Kingdom, played a role in promoting Irish products and culture on a global scale.

The economic growth of the Celtic Tiger era brought about tangible improvements in living standards for many Irish citizens. Unemployment rates declined, wages increased, and consumer spending surged. The transformation of Ireland's image from a struggling economy to an economic success story boosted national confidence and pride.

However, the period was not without its challenges. Rapid economic growth led to issues such as inflation, housing shortages, and environmental concerns. The bursting of the property bubble in the late 2000s marked the end of the Celtic Tiger era and exposed the vulnerabilities of an economy heavily reliant on construction and real estate.

The global financial crisis of 2008 had a profound impact on Ireland's economy. The collapse of the property market and the subsequent banking crisis led to a severe recession. The government's bailout of major banks and the implementation of austerity measures were necessary steps to stabilize the economy, but they also had significant social and political implications.

The Celtic Tiger era left a lasting impact on Ireland's economic, social, and cultural landscape. It transformed the country from an agrarian economy into a global player in technology, finance, and international trade. The period highlighted both the opportunities and challenges of globalization and underscored the importance of sustainable economic practices and prudent governance.

The legacy of the Celtic Tiger era continues to influence Ireland's economic policies and aspirations. It serves as a reminder of the potential for growth and innovation, but also the need for vigilance in ensuring that economic progress is balanced, inclusive, and resilient in the face of global uncertainties.

Good Friday Agreement: A Landmark for Peace in Northern Ireland

The Good Friday Agreement, also known as the Belfast Agreement, stands as a watershed moment in the history of Northern Ireland, marking a significant step towards ending decades of violence and conflict. This chapter delves into the origins, intricacies, and enduring impact of this landmark peace accord.

The roots of the Good Friday Agreement can be traced back to the 1980s when efforts to find a peaceful resolution to the conflict gained momentum. The persistent violence, suffering, and social divisions spurred leaders on both sides to seek a lasting solution. International involvement, particularly from the United States, played a pivotal role in facilitating negotiations and encouraging dialogue.

The agreement, officially reached on April 10, 1998, was the culmination of intense negotiations involving political parties in Northern Ireland, the British and Irish governments, and international mediators. It aimed to address the fundamental issues that had fueled the conflict—governance, policing, decommissioning of weapons, and justice.

One of the central tenets of the Good Friday Agreement was the establishment of a power-sharing government in Northern Ireland. The Northern Ireland Assembly and Executive were designed to include representatives from both Unionist and Nationalist communities, ensuring that all voices were heard in the governance of the region.

The issue of policing and justice was another critical aspect of the agreement. A new Police Service of Northern Ireland (PSNI) was established, aimed at building a police force that was representative of the diverse community and enjoyed the trust of all citizens. The Independent Commission on Policing for Northern Ireland (Patten Commission) played a significant role in shaping the new police service.

Perhaps one of the most challenging aspects of the agreement was the decommissioning of paramilitary weapons. The commitment to disarmament was a key step towards building trust between the communities. The Independent International Commission on Decommissioning (IICD) oversaw the process of weapons decommissioning, although the issue remained contentious.

The Good Friday Agreement recognized the principle of consent, acknowledging that any change in Northern Ireland's constitutional status would require the consent of the majority. This signaled a shift towards a more inclusive and democratic approach to the region's future.

The agreement also addressed the sensitive issue of prisoners and the release of those convicted of Troubles-related crimes. The release of prisoners was a complex and emotional topic, but it was deemed necessary to build a bridge towards reconciliation and peace.

The legacy of the Good Friday Agreement is multi-faceted. While it did not resolve all the issues or completely erase the scars of the past, it provided a framework for addressing grievances, fostering dialogue, and building a shared future. The peace process that ensued marked a transformative period for Northern Ireland, as communities that had been divided for generations began to bridge the gap and work towards a common vision.

The period following the agreement witnessed significant progress. Paramilitary violence significantly diminished, and the power-sharing institutions were established. However, the process was not without challenges, and the suspension of the institutions at various points highlighted the ongoing tensions and complexities of reconciliation.

The Good Friday Agreement remains relevant in the present day, as the people of Northern Ireland continue to grapple with the legacies of the past and navigate the complexities of their shared history. It serves as a testament to the power of dialogue, compromise, and the pursuit of peace, reminding us that even in the face of deep-seated divisions, a path towards reconciliation and stability is possible.

Shaping the European Stage: Ireland's Role in the EU

Ireland's relationship with the European Union (EU) has been a pivotal aspect of its modern history, with significant implications for its economy, politics, and identity. This chapter delves into the evolution of Ireland's role within the EU, exploring the factors that shaped its engagement and the impact it has had on both the nation and the broader European stage.

Ireland's journey within the EU began in 1973 when it officially joined the European Economic Community (EEC), the precursor to the EU. The decision to join marked a significant shift in Ireland's economic and political orientation, as the nation sought to overcome its historical isolation and leverage the benefits of European integration.

Economic transformation was a key driving force behind Ireland's embrace of the EU. The nation's economy underwent a radical shift, transitioning from an agrarian-based economy to a more diversified and export-oriented one. EU membership provided access to a vast common market, enabling Irish businesses to expand their reach and attract foreign investment.

The EU also played a crucial role in supporting Ireland's development through financial aid and structural funds. The Common Agricultural Policy (CAP) provided crucial support to Ireland's agricultural sector, while regional development funds helped boost infrastructure and economic growth in less-developed areas.

Ireland's relationship with the EU was not without its challenges. The nation's stance on various EU policies, such as the Common Fisheries Policy, often reflected its unique interests and circumstances. Additionally, referendums on key EU treaties, such as the Lisbon Treaty in 2009, highlighted the complexity of striking a balance between national sovereignty and European integration.

The Good Friday Agreement of 1998, which helped bring an end to the conflict in Northern Ireland, was also facilitated by the EU. The support and funding provided by the EU played a vital role in helping to underpin the peace process and promote cross-border cooperation.

Ireland's role within the EU extended beyond economic and political matters. The nation actively participated in EU institutions and initiatives, contributing to policy discussions and decision-making processes. Irish politicians and officials took on roles within the European Parliament, the European Commission, and other EU bodies, helping to shape the direction of the Union as a whole.

One of the defining moments in Ireland's EU journey was the financial crisis of 2008 and the subsequent bailout in 2010. The nation's economy, which had experienced rapid growth during the Celtic Tiger years, suffered a severe downturn. The bailout, which included assistance from the EU, the International Monetary Fund (IMF), and the European Central Bank (ECB), marked a challenging period for Ireland and highlighted the interdependence of EU member states' economies.

The Brexit process introduced a new dimension to Ireland's relationship with the EU. The potential impact of a UK withdrawal from the EU, particularly in relation to the border between Northern Ireland and the Republic of Ireland, became a central concern. The EU played a significant role in brokering the Northern Ireland Protocol, which aimed to prevent a hard border on the island of Ireland.

Ireland's role within the EU continues to evolve in the 21st century. The nation's commitment to European values, its contributions to policy discussions, and its pursuit of economic growth and social progress remain central to its engagement with the Union. As Ireland navigates the challenges and opportunities of a rapidly changing world, its relationship with the EU will continue to shape its future trajectory on both the national and European stages.

A Changing Faith: Religion in Contemporary Irish Society

Religion has long been a central and intricate facet of Irish identity, culture, and social fabric. However, the latter part of the 20th century and the beginning of the 21st century have witnessed profound shifts in the role and influence of religion within Irish society. This chapter delves into the evolving landscape of religion in modern Ireland, examining the factors that have contributed to change and the impact of these transformations on the nation's identity and values.

Historically, Ireland's religious landscape was dominated by the Roman Catholic Church. The Church's influence extended across various aspects of Irish life, including education, healthcare, and social welfare. Catholicism played a crucial role in shaping moral values, guiding social norms, and connecting individuals to their heritage.

The latter part of the 20th century, however, marked a turning point. Scandals and controversies, including revelations of clerical abuse, led to a decline in the Church's moral authority and a significant loss of trust among the faithful. These revelations shook the foundations of a religious institution that had been deeply embedded in Irish society for centuries.

As a result of these scandals, a decline in Church attendance became apparent. Younger generations, in particular, exhibited a departure from traditional religious practices. The once-ubiquitous presence of nuns, priests, and religious figures in schools, hospitals, and communities began to wane. Many individuals sought to distance themselves from an institution they perceived as out of touch or tarnished.

In tandem with these developments, Ireland's society became more diverse and multicultural due to immigration and globalization. This diversity brought with it an array of religious beliefs and practices, contributing to a pluralistic religious landscape. Islam, Hinduism, Buddhism, and other faiths began to find a place within Irish society, reshaping the religious tapestry and adding to the complexity of Ireland's identity.

The influence of religion on social and political issues also underwent transformation. Topics such as divorce, contraception, and same-sex marriage sparked debates that challenged the Church's traditional teachings and positions. The successful 2015 referendum legalizing same-sex marriage illustrated the evolving attitudes of Irish citizens toward social issues that had once been dominated by religious perspectives.

While the Catholic Church's influence waned, it would be an oversimplification to declare a complete decline of faith in Ireland. Many individuals and communities continue to find solace, meaning, and purpose in their religious beliefs. A segment of the population remains dedicated to their faith, and traditional religious practices such as baptisms, weddings, and funerals remain significant life events for many.

Moreover, efforts to address the wrongdoings of the past and foster transparency within the Catholic Church have been ongoing. Reforms and initiatives aimed at acknowledging and redressing the harms caused by clerical abuse have been introduced, reflecting a desire for accountability and renewal.

The relationship between religion and Irish identity continues to evolve. The narrative of Irish identity has become more inclusive, recognizing the diverse array of beliefs and values that contribute to the nation's cultural mosaic. Religion, once an integral marker of Irish identity, now coexists with an array of cultural, ethnic, and personal identifiers that shape the contemporary Irish experience.

As Ireland navigates the complexities of modernity, globalization, and cultural diversity, religion remains a pivotal factor in the ongoing construction of its national identity. The transformations in the religious landscape reflect the broader journey of a nation reconciling its rich history with the evolving aspirations of its citizens in a rapidly changing world.

Gaelic Revival: Resurgence of Language and Heritage

The Gaelic Revival stands as a vibrant chapter in Ireland's history, marked by a determined effort to rejuvenate and celebrate the Irish language, culture, and heritage. This resurgence, spanning the late 19th and early 20th centuries, was a response to centuries of colonial influence and suppression, aiming to reclaim a distinct Irish identity that had been marginalized.

Language has always been a cornerstone of culture, acting as a vessel for transmitting tradition, stories, and shared experiences. The Gaelic language, also known as Irish, was deeply woven into the fabric of Irish society for centuries. However, the imposition of English by colonial powers, coupled with socio-economic pressures, led to a decline in the use of Gaelic as a spoken language.

The Gaelic Revival emerged as a response to this linguistic erosion, championing the revitalization of the Irish language as a means of preserving and expressing national identity. Pioneers of the revival, such as Douglas Hyde and Eoin MacNeill, believed that language was the key to reconnecting with the rich cultural heritage of the past and forging a path towards a distinct Irish future.

Efforts to promote the Irish language encompassed various spheres, including education, literature, and the arts. The establishment of the Gaelic League (Conradh na Gaeilge) in 1893 was a pivotal development. The organization aimed to popularize the use of Irish and to create a sense of pride and ownership among Irish speakers. The league organized language classes, cultural events, and festivals, creating a vibrant space for the Irish language to thrive.

The literary movement also played an instrumental role in the Gaelic Revival. Writers like W.B. Yeats, Lady Gregory, and J.M. Synge sought inspiration from Gaelic folklore, myths, and history, incorporating these elements into their works. The Abbey Theatre, founded by Lady Gregory and W.B. Yeats in 1904, provided a platform for showcasing Irish plays and promoting indigenous talent.

The revival of traditional music and dance further contributed to the rejuvenation of Irish culture. Traditional instruments such as the fiddle, harp, and bodhrán experienced a resurgence, and Irish dance gained prominence on both national and international stages. The popularity of traditional music festivals, céilís, and Irish dance performances reflected a reconnection with cultural roots.

The Gaelic Revival extended beyond cultural and artistic realms, influencing political aspirations as well. The revival of language and heritage was closely intertwined with the quest for national self-determination and independence. The sentiment that cultural reawakening was essential for asserting Irish identity and asserting political autonomy gained traction.

The Gaelic Revival's influence on Irish society was enduring. While the Irish language did not fully supplant English, it did experience a resurgence in usage, particularly in certain pockets of the country. The movement succeeded in fostering a sense of pride in Irish heritage, establishing cultural institutions, and creating a space for indigenous cultural expression to flourish.

The impact of the Gaelic Revival resonates even in contemporary times. Cultural initiatives, language preservation efforts, and the celebration of Gaelic heritage remain an integral part of Irish society. The Irish language holds official status in the Republic of Ireland, and there are ongoing efforts to promote bilingualism and revitalize Irish as a living language.

The Gaelic Revival stands as a testament to the resilience of a people determined to reclaim their cultural heritage and assert their identity. It serves as a reminder that culture and language are essential components of a nation's identity, connecting the present to the past and shaping the trajectory of its future.

Green Innovation: Ireland's Commitment to Sustainability

In an era marked by growing environmental concerns and the urgency of addressing climate change, Ireland's dedication to sustainability and green innovation has taken center stage. This chapter delves into Ireland's journey towards a more sustainable future, examining the initiatives, policies, and advancements that have solidified its commitment to environmental stewardship and green innovation.

Ireland's transformation towards a greener future gained momentum in the late 20th century, driven by a growing awareness of the environmental challenges facing the planet. The nation's rich natural beauty and dependence on natural resources highlighted the importance of safeguarding its unique landscapes, biodiversity, and ecosystems.

The early steps towards sustainability focused on the preservation of natural habitats and the reduction of pollution. Initiatives such as the establishment of national parks and protected areas, such as the Burren in County Clare and Killarney National Park in County Kerry, were instrumental in conserving Ireland's natural heritage.

In recent decades, Ireland has shifted its focus to embracing renewable energy sources and reducing greenhouse gas emissions. The nation's abundant wind and ocean resources have positioned it as a leader in renewable energy. Wind farms, both onshore and offshore, have proliferated across the country, contributing significantly to the renewable energy mix.

Ireland's transition to renewable energy was further exemplified by its commitment to offshore wind energy. Projects like the Arklow Bank Wind Park and the Codling Wind Park have the potential to transform Ireland's energy landscape and significantly reduce reliance on fossil fuels.

Additionally, advancements in solar energy, bioenergy, and hydropower have diversified Ireland's renewable energy portfolio. The government's Renewable Energy Action Plan outlined ambitious targets for the expansion of these sectors, with the aim of achieving 70% renewable electricity by 2030.

The transportation sector, a significant contributor to greenhouse gas emissions, has also witnessed innovation towards sustainability. The Electric Vehicle (EV) charging network has been expanding, incentivizing the adoption of EVs and reducing carbon emissions from transport. Moreover, investment in public transportation, cycling infrastructure, and pedestrian-friendly urban planning has been prioritized to reduce reliance on private cars.

Efforts to enhance energy efficiency in buildings have been central to Ireland's sustainability agenda. The introduction of building regulations and incentives for energy-efficient construction have led to the emergence of green building practices. Retrofitting existing buildings with energy-efficient technologies has also gained momentum, contributing to a reduction in energy consumption.

Ireland's commitment to sustainability extends to waste management and circular economy principles. The introduction of plastic bag levies and initiatives to reduce single-use plastics have aimed to mitigate environmental degradation. Recycling programs, waste-to-energy facilities, and composting initiatives have been established to minimize the impact of waste on the environment.

The agricultural sector, a cornerstone of Ireland's economy, has also embraced sustainable practices. Initiatives to improve soil health, reduce chemical inputs, and promote sustainable farming techniques reflect a commitment to balancing agricultural productivity with environmental conservation.

Ireland's role in global environmental efforts is not to be underestimated. The nation's participation in international agreements like the Paris Agreement and its support for the United Nations Sustainable Development Goals underscore its dedication to a global green agenda.

The journey towards sustainability is ongoing, and Ireland's green innovation continues to evolve. The nation's commitment to phasing out fossil fuels, embracing renewable energy, and fostering sustainable practices across sectors showcases its dedication to safeguarding the planet for future generations. The strides made in green innovation exemplify Ireland's potential to be a catalyst for positive change in the global pursuit of a more sustainable and resilient future.

Wildlife Wonders: Exploring Flora and Fauna Across the Land

Ireland's diverse landscapes and varied ecosystems offer a haven for a rich array of flora and fauna, making it a captivating destination for nature enthusiasts and conservationists alike. This chapter embarks on a journey through the intricate web of life that thrives across the Emerald Isle, showcasing the remarkable wildlife wonders that call Ireland home.

The island's varied geography, from lush forests to rugged coastlines, provides a range of habitats that support a diverse range of plant and animal species. Ireland's relatively mild climate, influenced by the Atlantic Ocean, further contributes to its biodiversity, allowing both native and migratory species to thrive.

Forests are a defining feature of Ireland's landscape, and they harbor a wealth of biodiversity. Ancient woodlands, such as Killarney's oak forests, provide a home to species like red deer, pine martens, and a variety of bird species. In contrast, the Burren's limestone landscape supports unique plants such as the Arctic-alpine species and rare orchids.

Ireland's water bodies, including lakes, rivers, and coastal areas, teem with life. The otter, a symbol of clean water and healthy ecosystems, can be found in various freshwater habitats. Rivers and lakes are also home to species such as salmon, trout, and the critically endangered freshwater pearl mussel.

The coastline stretching over 3,000 kilometers offers vital habitats for marine life. Seabird colonies are a prominent feature, with species like puffins, gannets, and terns nesting along the cliffs and rocky shores. Grey seals and harbor seals inhabit coastal waters, while dolphins and whales are frequent visitors, adding to Ireland's reputation as a prime whale-watching destination.

Wetlands play a critical role in supporting biodiversity, serving as habitats for various bird species and wetland plants. The Corncrake, a secretive bird known for its distinctive call, finds refuge in Ireland's wet grasslands. Protected areas like the Shannon Callows and Wexford Wildfowl Reserve provide sanctuaries for these species.

Bogs, iconic landscapes of Ireland, house unique flora and fauna adapted to their acidic and waterlogged conditions. Carnivorous plants like the sundew and butterwort thrive here, along with dragonflies, frogs, and lizards. The raised bogs of Ireland are particularly important for their role in carbon storage and preserving ancient plant material.

Conservation efforts have been instrumental in safeguarding Ireland's wildlife wonders. National parks and reserves, such as Glenveagh National Park and Connemara National Park, provide protected spaces for species to flourish. Initiatives to restore and rehabilitate habitats, as well as promote sustainable land management, play a pivotal role in preserving Ireland's natural heritage.

The challenges facing Ireland's wildlife are not to be ignored. Habitat loss, pollution, invasive species, and climate change pose threats to native flora and fauna. The introduction of non-native species like the grey squirrel and

Japanese knotweed can have detrimental impacts on native ecosystems.

The passion for wildlife conservation has led to the emergence of numerous organizations dedicated to preserving Ireland's biodiversity. The Irish Wildlife Trust, BirdWatch Ireland, and An Taisce are just a few examples of groups actively working to protect and restore habitats, raise awareness, and advocate for policy changes that prioritize nature.

Ireland's commitment to biodiversity is reflected in its designation as a UNESCO Global Geopark and its participation in international conservation agreements. The nation's engagement in efforts to combat climate change and its dedication to achieving sustainable development further underline its role in safeguarding the planet's precious natural resources.

Exploring Ireland's flora and fauna is an adventure that unveils the intricate interconnectedness of life on the island. The diversity of species, the resilience of ecosystems, and the collective efforts towards conservation highlight the irreplaceable value of Ireland's wildlife wonders. Amid the challenges of a changing world, Ireland's commitment to preserving its natural heritage is a testament to its determination to ensure a harmonious coexistence between humans and the remarkable creatures that inhabit the land.

Tastes of the Island: Culinary Traditions and Modern Cuisine

Ireland's culinary journey is a delightful exploration of traditions, flavors, and modern innovation. This chapter delves into the rich tapestry of Irish cuisine, tracing its roots from ancient practices to the contemporary culinary landscape that marries tradition with modern flair.

Culinary traditions in Ireland are deeply interwoven with the island's history, geography, and cultural heritage. The rugged landscapes and maritime influence have played a pivotal role in shaping traditional dishes. Staples like potatoes, seafood, dairy, and meats formed the core of the Irish diet, providing sustenance for generations.

Potatoes, often referred to as the "Irish staple," were central to the diet from the 18th to the 19th century. The Great Famine of the mid-19th century, which devastated the potato crop, had profound effects on Irish society and immigration patterns. The legacy of the potato remains significant, as it's an enduring symbol of Irish resilience.

Seafood, sourced from the abundant surrounding waters, is another pillar of Irish cuisine. Salmon, mackerel, and haddock are staples, enjoyed in traditional dishes like smoked salmon and fisherman's pie. Oysters, particularly from the Galway region, are prized delicacies enjoyed both locally and internationally.

Dairy products hold a special place in Irish cuisine, with butter and cheese being integral components. Irish butter, known for its rich flavor and distinct golden hue, is celebrated in both traditional and contemporary recipes. Irish farmhouse cheeses have garnered international recognition for their quality and variety.

Meat has also been a cornerstone of Irish cooking. Traditional dishes like Irish stew, made with lamb or mutton, and corned beef, often enjoyed on St. Patrick's Day, showcase the importance of meat in Irish culinary heritage. The practice of curing and preserving meats for the winter months has ancient origins.

In recent decades, Irish cuisine has experienced a renaissance driven by a renewed interest in local and seasonal ingredients, as well as global culinary trends. Modern Irish chefs have garnered acclaim for their creativity and innovation, blending traditional recipes with modern techniques and presentation.

Farm-to-table practices have gained traction, with a focus on locally sourced ingredients. Artisanal producers, farmers' markets, and sustainable farming practices have become integral to the contemporary Irish culinary scene. This approach reflects a conscious effort to honor traditional flavors while embracing a more sustainable and ethical approach to food production.

Dublin's culinary scene has evolved to cater to diverse tastes, with a myriad of international cuisines available alongside traditional Irish fare. The city's food festivals, such as the Taste of Dublin, celebrate this culinary diversity and offer a platform for chefs and producers to showcase their creations.

The craft beer and whiskey renaissance has also been a notable development in Ireland's culinary landscape. Microbreweries and distilleries have proliferated, contributing to the revival of traditional brewing methods and the creation of innovative, high-quality products.

The reimagining of traditional dishes is evident in the work of Michelin-starred restaurants that put a contemporary twist on classic Irish flavors. Dishes like modern interpretations of boxty (a potato pancake) and artisanal black pudding highlight the creativity that flourishes in Ireland's culinary arts.

Ireland's culinary evolution has not gone unnoticed on the international stage. The island's reputation as a food destination has grown, attracting food enthusiasts from around the world. The prestigious World's 50 Best Restaurants list has recognized Irish culinary excellence, further solidifying the nation's place in the global gastronomic scene.

As Ireland's culinary journey continues, the marriage of tradition and modernity remains at its heart. The preservation of centuries-old recipes and practices, coupled with the embrace of contemporary techniques and global influences, defines the exciting tapestry of flavors that is modern Irish cuisine. The taste of the island is a reflection of its history, culture, and the creative spirit of its culinary artists, offering a palate-pleasing experience that resonates with both locals and visitors alike.

Treasures of the Past: Unveiling Ireland's Historic Sites

Ireland's landscape is a living tapestry of history, adorned with countless historic sites that bear witness to the nation's rich and diverse past. This chapter invites you on a journey through time, exploring the treasures of the past that are woven into the fabric of Ireland's heritage.

Ancient structures stand as testament to Ireland's prehistoric origins. The passage tombs of Brú na Bóinne, including Newgrange and Knowth, are among the oldest and most intricate Neolithic structures in the world. Dating back over 5,000 years, these monuments offer insights into the rituals and beliefs of Ireland's earliest inhabitants.

Celtic heritage is vividly preserved in Ireland's historic sites. The Hill of Tara, once the seat of the High Kings of Ireland, is a place of immense archaeological and mythological significance. The standing stones and earthworks evoke a sense of the past, where ancient rituals and ceremonies unfolded.

Medieval castles, fortresses, and monasteries punctuate the Irish landscape, each with a unique story to tell. Dublin Castle, founded by the Normans, reflects Ireland's medieval past and served as a hub of power and governance. Blarney Castle in County Cork, with its famed Blarney Stone, is a cherished site for those seeking the "gift of gab."

Monastic settlements are a testament to Ireland's deep spiritual history. Glendalough, nestled in the Wicklow

Mountains, is renowned for its early Christian monastery founded by St. Kevin. The round towers, churches, and crosses that remain convey the devotion and craftsmanship of centuries past.

The medieval city of Kilkenny boasts Kilkenny Castle, a striking example of Anglo-Norman architecture. This castle, with its ornate interiors and sprawling grounds, provides a glimpse into the lifestyle of Ireland's aristocracy during the Middle Ages.

Ireland's strategic location made it a focal point of Viking activity. The Viking Triangle in Waterford showcases the influence of these seafaring invaders, with remains of walls, houses, and artifacts that speak to their presence and impact on Irish society.

Norman influences are visible in Ireland's landscape through the architecture of castles and cathedrals. Trim Castle in County Meath, the largest Norman castle in Ireland, stands as a formidable stronghold. The Rock of Cashel, an ancient fortress with religious significance, showcases the merging of Celtic and Norman cultures.

The rugged west coast is adorned with remnants of defensive tower houses and fortified towns. Bunratty Castle, one of the most complete medieval castles in Ireland, welcomes visitors to step back in time to the era of knights and banquets.

Ireland's recent history is also commemorated through historic sites. Kilmainham Gaol in Dublin bears witness to the struggle for Irish independence, having housed political prisoners during key moments in the nation's fight for self-determination.

These treasures of the past are not mere relics; they are living connections to Ireland's history and culture. The wealth of historic sites throughout the island reflects the continuity of human experience, bridging the gap between past and present. As you explore these sites, you embark on a journey through time, gaining insights into the diverse layers of Ireland's story and discovering the remarkable threads that have shaped its identity.

Dublin: Heart of the Republic: A Capital Rich in History

Dublin, the vibrant capital of Ireland, pulsates with a captivating blend of history, culture, and modernity. This chapter invites you to explore the layers of Dublin's past, a city that has played a pivotal role in shaping the nation's history and identity.

Dublin's origins trace back to the Viking Age, when it was established as a trading settlement called "Dubh Linn." The Vikings left their mark on the city, evident in artifacts and archaeological finds that unearth stories of their presence along the banks of the River Liffey.

Medieval Dublin blossomed into a center of commerce and culture. The medieval heart of the city, centered around Dublin Castle and Christ Church Cathedral, reveals a tapestry of narrow streets, medieval architecture, and historical landmarks. The magnificent St. Patrick's Cathedral, with its soaring spires and rich history, stands as a testament to Dublin's religious and architectural heritage.

Trinity College Dublin, founded in 1592, stands as a beacon of learning and scholarship. Its Old Library houses the Book of Kells, a beautifully illuminated manuscript that showcases the intricate craftsmanship and artistic skill of the early Christian era.

Dublin's connection to the struggle for Irish independence is deeply embedded in its streets and buildings. The General Post Office (GPO) on O'Connell Street, a focal point during the 1916 Easter Rising, holds immense historical significance. The Proclamation of the Irish Republic was read from its steps, marking a pivotal moment in the quest for self-determination.

Georgian Dublin, characterized by its elegant townhouses and leafy squares, flourished during the 18th century. Merrion Square and Fitzwilliam Square offer glimpses into the city's grand architectural past. Dublin's Georgian architecture reflects its position as a center of British influence during this period.

Dublin's literary heritage is a cherished aspect of the city's identity. It was home to literary giants like James Joyce, W.B. Yeats, and Samuel Beckett. The city's streets and neighborhoods come alive with references from Joyce's "Ulysses," inviting readers to traverse the same paths as its iconic characters.

The River Liffey, flowing through the heart of the city, has long been a source of inspiration and connection. Bridges like Ha'penny Bridge and Samuel Beckett Bridge not only facilitate movement but also symbolize the city's link between its historic and modern aspects.

Dublin's modern identity thrives alongside its historic roots. Temple Bar, a lively cultural quarter, is a hub for arts, music, and entertainment. The National Museum of Ireland showcases the country's archaeological treasures, while the Dublin Writers Museum pays homage to its literary legacy.

Dublin's role as the political and economic hub of the Republic is evident in its institutions and landmarks. The seat of the Irish government, Leinster House, is situated in the city center. The bustling Grafton Street offers premier shopping and a vibrant street atmosphere, embodying Dublin's contemporary allure.

The Dublin of today is a harmonious blend of tradition and innovation. From the echoes of Viking settlers to the spirit of revolution and the pursuit of creative expression, the city's streets, buildings, and stories encapsulate the essence of Ireland's journey through time. As you stroll through Dublin's neighborhoods, you navigate a living history that celebrates the past, embraces the present, and paves the way for the future of the vibrant capital at the heart of the Republic.

Belfast: From Industry to Identity: The Story of Northern Ireland's City

Belfast, the capital of Northern Ireland, is a city whose history is deeply intertwined with industry, identity, and a complex tapestry of cultural narratives. This chapter delves into the evolution of Belfast, tracing its journey from a thriving industrial hub to a city that embodies the multifaceted identity of Northern Ireland.

Belfast's roots are anchored in its strategic location on the banks of the River Lagan. Its proximity to natural resources and navigable waters led to its emergence as a center of trade and commerce during the 17th and 18th centuries. Shipbuilding, linen production, and trade flourished, laying the foundation for the city's industrial prowess.

The 19th century witnessed the rise of Belfast as a global shipbuilding and manufacturing powerhouse. The construction of the RMS Titanic at the Harland and Wolff shipyard epitomized the city's reputation as the "workshop of the world." Shipbuilding not only fueled economic growth but also shaped the social fabric of Belfast.

Belfast's industrial boom attracted a diverse population, including workers from across Ireland and beyond. The city's demographic landscape was characterized by a mix of Protestant and Catholic communities. However, religious tensions simmered beneath the surface, leading to periods of social unrest and division.

The early 20th century marked a turning point in Belfast's history. The political turmoil of Ireland's struggle for independence reverberated in the city. The partition of Ireland in 1921 resulted in the creation of Northern Ireland, with Belfast as its capital. This political division deepened the sectarian divide, shaping the identity and dynamics of the city for decades to come.

Turbulent times, such as the period known as "The Troubles," cast a shadow over Belfast's streets. The conflict between unionists and nationalists led to violence, upheaval, and a sense of uncertainty that gripped the city for over three decades. The Good Friday Agreement of 1998 brought a ceasefire and marked a turning point towards peace and reconciliation.

Belfast's transformation into a modern city with a renewed sense of identity and purpose has been notable. The city has embraced its cultural heritage and has emerged as a vibrant hub for arts, music, and literature. The Cathedral Quarter, with its galleries, theaters, and pubs, pulsates with creativity and expression.

Titanic Belfast, an iconic visitor attraction, pays homage to the city's shipbuilding legacy and the ill-fated Titanic's connection to Belfast. This interactive museum is a testament to Belfast's ability to preserve its industrial heritage while embracing innovation.

Belfast's architecture reflects its layered history. Victorian and Edwardian buildings stand alongside modern structures that symbolize the city's regeneration. The transformation of the Titanic Quarter, once a shipyard, into a mixed-use development showcases Belfast's capacity to reimagine its urban landscape.

The Belfast Peace Walls, erected during the Troubles, still stand as physical reminders of division. However, strides have been made to promote reconciliation, community development, and a shared vision for a peaceful future.

Today, Belfast is a city that looks to the future while acknowledging its past. The city's identity is no longer solely defined by its industrial legacy or political struggles; it's a tapestry woven with threads of resilience, creativity, and a commitment to shaping a more inclusive and unified future. As Belfast continues to evolve, it serves as a microcosm of Northern Ireland's complex journey toward identity, reconciliation, and a collective aspiration for a better tomorrow.

Galway: Where Tradition Meets the Atlantic: A Cultural Gem

Galway, a charming city perched on the western coast of Ireland, is a cultural gem that seamlessly marries tradition with the untamed beauty of the Atlantic Ocean. This chapter invites you to explore the rich tapestry of Galway's heritage, where history, music, language, and natural landscapes converge in a symphony of cultural vibrancy.

Galway's roots trace back to medieval times when it was a thriving port and trading hub. Its location along the Wild Atlantic Way made it a gateway for trade and communication with the wider world. The city's name "Gaillimh" is derived from the Irish word for "stony river," a nod to the River Corrib that meanders through its heart.

Cultural diversity is embedded in Galway's DNA. Its history as a trading port attracted merchants, adventurers, and settlers from various corners of the globe. This eclectic mix of influences is reflected in the city's architecture, from medieval stone walls to colorful Georgian facades.

The Claddagh, a historic fishing village within Galway, is known for the Claddagh ring—a symbol of love, friendship, and loyalty. Its maritime heritage is celebrated in the annual Galway Hooker Races, where traditional wooden sailing boats compete in a lively regatta.

Galway's cultural significance extends to its role as the European Capital of Culture in 2020, an honor that showcased its commitment to the arts and creativity. The city's year-long program of events celebrated local talent and global connections, leaving a lasting legacy on its cultural scene.

The Galway Arts Festival, held annually, transforms the city into a canvas of artistic expression. Theatrical performances, visual arts, music, and literature converge in a celebration that encapsulates Galway's dedication to nurturing creativity.

The Irish language, or "Gaeilge," is a cornerstone of Galway's identity. The city is a bastion of Gaeltacht culture, where the language thrives in everyday life. The annual Oireachtas na Gaeilge festival celebrates the Irish language through music, dance, and poetry.

Traditional Irish music reverberates through Galway's narrow streets and cozy pubs. The city is a magnet for musicians and enthusiasts alike. Quays Street, affectionately known as the "Music Street of Galway," comes alive with melodies that harken back to Ireland's musical heritage.

Galway's connection to the Atlantic Ocean is profound. The city's coastline is a gateway to the rugged landscapes of Connemara and the Aran Islands. The Cliffs of Moher, though not within Galway's borders, are a short drive away and offer breathtaking views of the Atlantic's might.

Galway's food scene is an embodiment of its fusion of tradition and innovation. Traditional dishes like seafood chowder, Connemara lamb, and Galway Bay oysters pay homage to the city's maritime heritage. Meanwhile, contemporary restaurants and artisanal markets showcase Galway's embrace of culinary creativity.

Galway's warm and welcoming spirit is epitomized in its people. The Galway Races, a world-renowned horse racing event, attracts visitors from far and wide. It's a showcase of the city's hospitality and its ability to bring people together for a common love of sport and celebration.

Galway's cultural dynamism is a reflection of its resilience and commitment to preserving its heritage while embracing the future. The city stands as a testament to the beauty of cultural fusion, where tradition, language, music, and nature converge to create an experience that is both timeless and uniquely Galwegian. As you wander through Galway's streets, you'll discover a place where the spirit of the Atlantic is matched only by the indomitable spirit of its people.

Cork: Maritime Legacy and Rebel Spirit: Ireland's Southern Hub

Cork, nestled in the southern reaches of Ireland, is a city steeped in maritime heritage and a resolute rebel spirit that has left an indelible mark on the nation's history. This chapter unveils the layers of Cork's past and present, where the intersection of trade, rebellion, and cultural richness forms a captivating narrative.

Cork's maritime legacy traces back to its strategic location along the River Lee and its proximity to the Atlantic Ocean. The city's history is intertwined with seafaring endeavors, trade, and shipbuilding that have shaped its economic and social fabric for centuries.

The English Market, an iconic hub of food and commerce, has been a cornerstone of Cork's identity since the 18th century. The market's ornate architecture and vibrant atmosphere showcase the city's culinary heritage, with stalls offering fresh produce, artisanal products, and a taste of tradition.

Cork's history of rebellion and resistance dates back to the Battle of Kinsale in 1601, a pivotal moment in Irish history. The city's association with rebellion continued through the centuries, earning it the nickname "Rebel Cork." The Irish War of Independence and subsequent Civil War left their mark on Cork's streets, with historic sites like the Gaol bearing witness to these turbulent times.

The city's architectural landscape reflects its diverse history. St. Fin Barre's Cathedral, a masterpiece of Gothic Revival architecture, pays homage to Cork's patron saint. Elizabeth Fort, a 17th-century star-shaped fortress, is a tangible reminder of Cork's strategic importance and defensive past.

Cork's connection to the sea is celebrated in its annual Midsummer Festival, where the city's quayside transforms into a maritime haven. The festival commemorates Cork's maritime legacy with boat races, food markets, and cultural events that highlight the city's affinity for the sea.

Cork's cultural vibrancy is evident in its thriving arts scene. The Cork Opera House, founded in the 19th century, remains a hub for theatrical performances, opera, and musical events. The Crawford Art Gallery showcases Ireland's artistic heritage, while the Glucksman Gallery offers a contemporary perspective on visual arts.

University College Cork (UCC), founded in 1845, contributes to Cork's intellectual legacy. Its historic campus and modern facilities have nurtured generations of scholars, thinkers, and innovators, adding to the city's cultural tapestry.

Cork's festivals and events reflect its eclectic spirit. The Cork Jazz Festival, one of the oldest jazz festivals in Europe, brings a harmonious fusion of music to the city's streets. The Cork Film Festival showcases cinematic artistry, and the International Choral Festival celebrates the power of music to unite cultures.

Cork's local food scene is a reflection of its rich agricultural surroundings. The city's proximity to fertile farmlands and the sea has inspired a culinary scene that marries tradition with innovation. Dishes like traditional Cork buttered eggs and seafood chowder are culinary highlights that capture the essence of the region.

Cork's resilience and cultural depth are mirrored in its people. The city's independent spirit, evident in its rebellious history, remains alive in the contemporary pursuits of its residents. The strong sense of community and commitment to preserving Cork's unique heritage are tangible in every corner of the city.

Cork stands as a testament to the synergy between history and modernity, rebellion and tradition. Its maritime legacy and tenacious spirit are woven into the fabric of its streets, buildings, and stories. As you traverse the city, you'll uncover a place where the currents of the River Lee echo the flow of time itself, where maritime history mingles with a rebel heart that beats to the rhythm of Cork's unique identity.

Conclusion

As we bring our journey through the history of Ireland to a close, we find ourselves standing at the crossroads of time, where the past and present intersect to shape the nation's identity. Ireland's history is a symphony of triumphs and trials, cultural richness and complexity, all intertwined within its rugged landscapes and spirited people.

From the prehistoric foundations that laid the groundwork for Celtic culture, to the medieval monasteries that preserved knowledge during turbulent times, the threads of Ireland's past weave a tapestry that spans millennia. The rise of Gaelic power, the arrival of Vikings on Irish shores, the influences of Norman conquests, Tudor and Stuart plantations, and the impact of English Civil Wars are chapters that unfolded against the backdrop of Ireland's changing political and social landscapes.

The struggles for independence, from the Easter Rising to the War of Independence, shaped the course of Ireland's destiny, culminating in the establishment of the Republic. The Troubles, a period of conflict and division, cast a shadow over the nation, but the Good Friday Agreement marked a landmark for peace and reconciliation.

Throughout its history, Ireland's cultural heritage has remained steadfast, a beacon of resilience and creativity. The revival of literature, the resurgence of the Irish language, and the emergence of a vibrant art scene are testaments to the enduring spirit of the Irish people.

The modern chapters of Ireland's story include its role in the European Union, commitment to sustainability, evolving faith, and its global presence as a center of education, technology, and innovation. The cities, each with their own unique character, have played pivotal roles in shaping Ireland's past and present, from Dublin's political significance to Cork's maritime legacy and Galway's cultural vibrancy.

Ireland's history is not just a collection of facts; it's a living narrative that continues to evolve with each passing day. It's a tale of resilience, determination, and the unwavering spirit of a nation that has overcome adversity to find its place on the world stage. As we reflect on this journey, we are reminded that Ireland's story is far from over; it's a story that continues to be written by the generations that call this land home. With each new chapter, Ireland's legacy grows, adding to the rich tapestry that is its history.

We sincerely hope you've enjoyed delving into the fascinating history of Ireland through the pages of this book. Exploring the ancient origins, medieval tales, struggles, triumphs, and cultural riches that have shaped Ireland's journey has been a true honor.

If you found this book informative and engaging, we kindly ask for a moment of your time to leave a positive review. Your feedback not only helps us improve but also encourages others to embark on this historical journey with us.

Thank you for joining us on this exploration of Ireland's captivating history. Your support means the world to us, and we hope you'll continue to seek knowledge and inspiration through the pages of our books.

Printed in Great Britain
by Amazon